Grumpy Trumpy

A Bad Hombre Parody
By Stacey Russo

ANYONE BUT TRUMP 2020

For my friends and family, who would like to see America great again.
And for my daughter, Lila, who has taught me that love trumps all...and silly rhyming books are fun to read.

I was walking down the road and I saw...

Donald Trump,

Hee Haw!

And he complained about being the most unfairly treated politician in history.

He was a grumpy Trumpy.

I was walking down the road and I saw Donald Trump,

Hee Haw!

He complained about being the most unfairly treated politician in history...

and he wanted to build a large wall and make Mexico pay for it!

I was walking down the road and I saw Donald Trump,

Hee Haw!

He complained about being the most unfairly treated politician in history, he wanted to build a large wall and make Mexico pay for it...

and for some reason he was quite orange.

He was a
fake-n-bakey,
Humpty Dumpty,
grumpy Trumpy.

I was walking down the road and I saw Donald Trump,

Hee Haw!

He complained about being the most unfairly treated politician in history, he wanted to build a large wall and make Mexico pay for it, for some reason he was quite orange...

and he didn't respect women, Muslims, Mexicans, Democrats, journalists, or really anyone else.

He was a meanie weenie, fake-n-bakey, Humpty Dumpty, grumpy Trumpy.

I was walking down the road and I saw Donald Trump,

Hee Haw!

He complained about being the most unfairly treated politician in history, he wanted to build a large wall and make Mexico pay for it, for some reason he was quite orange, he didn't respect women, Muslims, Mexicans, Democrats, journalists, or really anyone else...

and he had the grammar of a 3rd grader.

He was a **scummy dummy**, meanie weenie,
fake-n-bakey, Humpty Dumpty, grumpy Trumpy.

I was walking down the road and I saw Donald Trump,

Hee Haw!

He complained about being the most unfairly treated politician in history, he wanted to build a large wall and make Mexico pay for it, for some reason he was quite orange, he didn't respect women, Muslims, Mexicans, Democrats, journalists, or really anyone else, he had the grammar of a 3rd grader...

and his personality was as appealing as his looks.

He was a frumpy dumpy, scummy dummy, meanie weenie, fake-n-bakey, Humpty Dumpty, grumpy Trumpy.

I was walking down the road and I saw Donald Trump,

Hee Haw!

He complained about being the most unfairly treated politician in history, he wanted to build a large wall and make Mexico pay for it, for some reason he was quite orange, he didn't respect women, Muslims, Mexicans, Democrats, journalists, or really anyone else, he had the grammar of a 3rd grader, his personality was as appealing as his looks...

and he changed his mind on important issues as it suited him.

The Best President in the World's Important Issues Cheat Sheet

For
- ~~pro-choice~~ pro-life
- Invade Syria
- play a lot of golf while president
- ~~gun control~~
- ~~accept refugees~~
- separate families
- Medicare/ Medicade cuts- "reforms"
- ~~LGBT rights~~
- ~~Drain the swamp! Lobbyists are okay~~
- China

Against
- ~~NATO- it's obsolete!~~
- ~~invade Syria~~
- ~~play a lot of golf while president~~
- ~~president~~
- gun control
- accept refugees
- ~~separate families~~
- ~~Medicare/ Medicade cuts~~
- LGBT rights
- ~~China~~

BORING!- I'll just tweet what I'm thinking

He was a **wishy-washy**, frumpy dumpy, scummy dummy, meanie weenie, fake-n-bakey, Humpty Dumpty, grumpy Trumpy.

I was walking down the road and I saw Donald Trump,

Hee Haw!

He complained about being the most unfairly treated politician in history, he wanted to build a large wall and make Mexico pay for it, for some reason he was quite orange, he didn't respect women, Muslims, Mexicans, Democrats, journalists, or really anyone else, he had the grammar of a 3rd grader, his personality was as appealing as his looks, he changed his mind on important issues as it suited him...

and he claimed he'd make America Great again when it was much better before him.

He was a phony baloney, wishy-washy, frumpy dumpy, scummy dummy, meanie weenie, fake-n-bakey, Humpty Dumpty, grumpy Trumpy.

I was walking down the road
and I saw Donald Trump...

Drain the swamp

Climate change is real

Printed in Poland
by Amazon Fulfillment
Poland Sp. z o.o., Wrocław

65081501R10016